MW01053199

Let's Talk About Feelings

What Is A Feeling?

Written by David W. Krueger, M.D., F.A.P.A.
Illustrated by Jean Whitney

Parenting Press, Inc.
Seattle, Washington

The author would like to express thanks to Mary Blount Christian and
Terry Dunnahoo for their help and support.

Cover design by Alice C. Merrill
Book design by Shari Steelsmith-Duffin

ISBN 0-943990-75-0 Paper
ISBN 0-943990-76-9 Library binding
LC 93-084652

Parenting Press, Inc.
P.O. Box 75267
Seattle, WA 98125

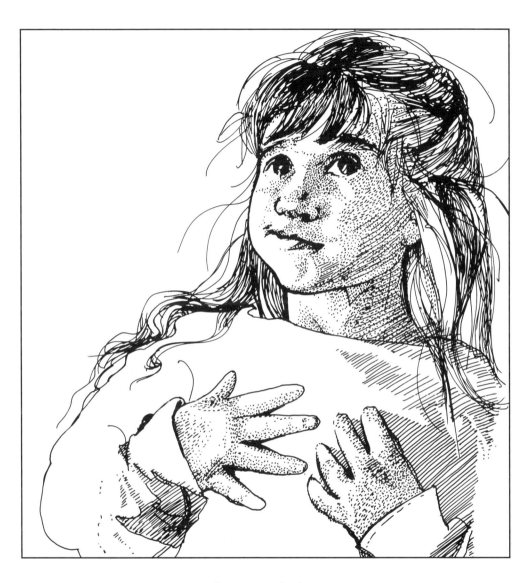

What is a feeling?
Is a feeling something I can touch?

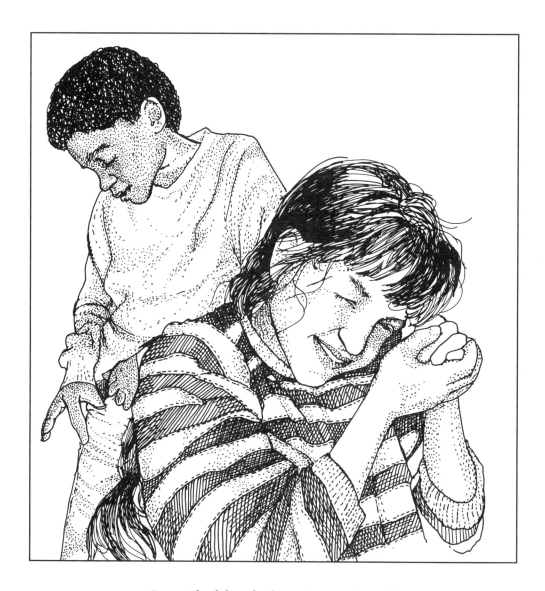

Can I hold a feeling in my hands?
Or carry one in my pocket with my truck?

Can I hear a feeling?
I hope it's not as loud as my baby sister's drum.

Can I taste a feeling?
I hope it tastes like ice cream and not like a worm.

Can I play with a feeling—like I play with my toys?

Can I throw it like a ball?
Or squeeze it like a sponge?

Can I see a feeling when I look around me?
Will someone give it to me like a present with a big bow?

What is a feeling? Feelings are the way I react
to what's happening to me and around me.
Some feelings I feel in my body.
Some feelings I feel in my heart and mind.

I can feel hurt in *two* different ways.
My body hurts when I fall off my bike and skin my knee.
And my heart and mind hurt when I feel left out
after someone ignores me.

I can feel good in *two* different ways.
My body feels good when I'm wrapped up in a big,
fluffy blanket, feeling all warm and snugly.
I feel good on the inside when my mom gives me
a goodnight kiss.

I feel sick when my head throbs,
and my bones ache, and my body is hot.
And I feel sick at heart when
I break my mom's favorite lamp.

Sometimes it's hard to find the right words for feelings.
I have so many feelings—
different ones at different times.

Other people have many feelings, too.
I can get clues to their feelings by what I see and hear.

I can tell that someone feels shy
when I see them sitting alone at a birthday party.

I can tell that my mom feels silly when she makes a funny face, or walks on her hands, or dances with a broom.
Let's talk about some other feelings
and get to know them better.

Excited is the feeling I get when something
really good is about to happen.
Like when tomorrow is my birthday!
Or when my favorite dessert is next and I've just
finished every last bite of my dinner.

Jealous is a sort of mad, sort of sad, yucky feeling.
Like when I get sent to my room
and my sister gets a hug.

Tired-but-good-all-over is the feeling
I have after I run and play hard.

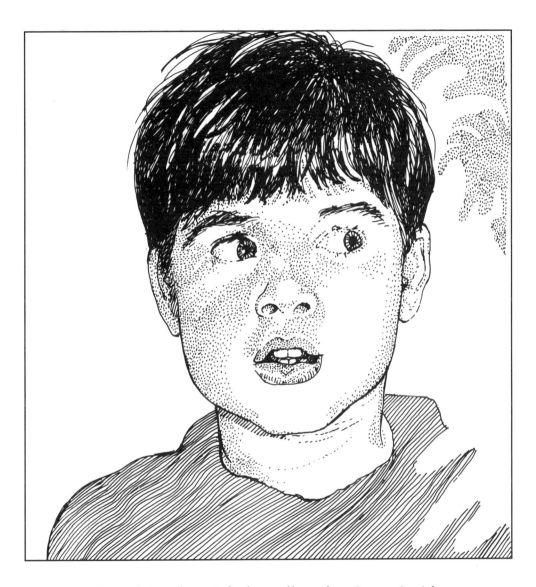

Scared is when I feel small and quivery inside;
my mind sees a picture of something
big, fierce, and awful.

Mad feels hot and bursting inside,
like when nothing works right,
and nobody does what *I* want them to do.

Guilty is a heavy feeling of worrying
when I've done something wrong—like lying.

Happy is when I laugh or smile—
when everything is going just right.
Sometimes it feels like I'm floating through the air.

Sad is a quiet and lost feeling,
like when my puppy is sick, and just
licks my fingers instead of playing with me.

Proud is what I feel when I've done something
all by myself! I feel bigger and taller
when I'm proud.

I don't have words or names for all of my feelings.
But sometimes I don't need words.

One thing is for sure.
Whatever feeling I have is special
because it's *real* and it's *mine*.

One of the most fundamental needs in a child's development is the ability to connect emotionally with his or her parents. It is essential for the child to feel understood. When these needs are met, a child feels whole and safe.

Children come to know themselves by how they feel. Learning to identify and understand their feelings builds a foundation for self-esteem and self-mastery.

As adults, we know that feelings are not tangible. How can we talk about an abstract concept with children who have not yet passed beyond thinking in a concrete manner? How can we help them take ownership of something they cannot hold?

What Is A Feeling? depicts and names a variety of feelings for children, through a read-together-and-talk-about-it series of questions and answers. This book can be used as a springboard to encourage children to describe their own vast world of feelings.

When children are able to acknowledge and accept all their different feelings—nobody is happy or sad all the time—they will be on the road to becoming confident adults.

David W. Krueger, M.D., F.A.P.A.

Fun with Feelings

1. Look in the mirror and make a face that expresses one of the feelings in the circle.

2. Describe a situation when you felt one of the feelings in the circle.

3. Make a face that expresses one of the feelings in the circle and have a friend guess which feeling it is.

4. Tell what you do when you feel one of the feelings in the circle.

5. Find all the feelings in the circle that you have felt today.

Parents and Teachers: Copy this circle on cardboard and attach a cardboard spinner with a brass fastener to the center. Invite several children to play the *Fun with Feelings* games together.

Game Circle for *Fun with Feelings*

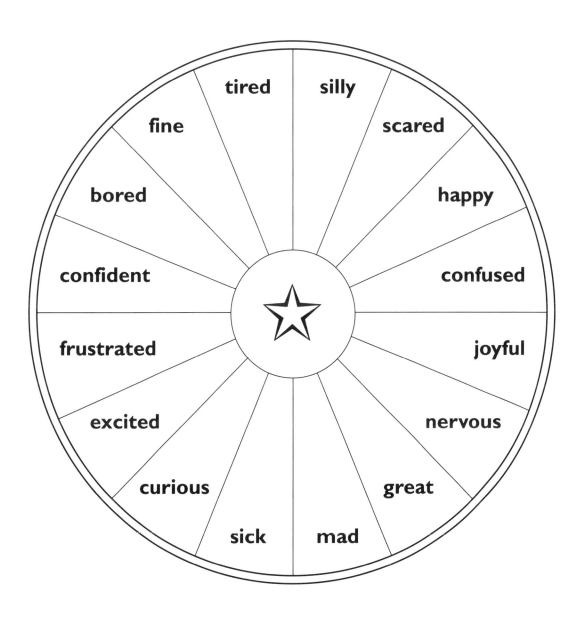

The Dealing With Feelings Series

Author Elizabeth Crary gives kids ideas for safe, creative ways to express their emotions. Each book features a choose-you-own-ending format, which encourages reader involvement and allows kids to discover, or invent for themselves positive, satisfying ways to express their feelings. *Ages 3-9, 32 pages, 7x8½, $5.95 paperback, illus.*

I'm Mad Readers help Katie find ways to express her anger, who move on to fill an afternoon with laughter and fun, instead of being mad all day.

I'm Frustrated When Alex can't learn to skate right away, readers help him find better ways to express his frustration and find other fun things to do.

I'm Proud Mandy learns to tie her shoes, but no one seems very excited.

I'm Furious When Matt's little brother ruins his best baseball card, readers help Matt choose constructive ways to handle his anger.

I'm Excited Annie and Jesse are super excited because it's their birthday.

I'm Scared Tracy is terrified of the new neighbor's big dog, and needs help deciding what to do about her feelings.

Let's Talk About Feelings Series

All My Feelings At Home: Ellie's Day

by Susan Levine Friedman and Susan Conlin
Five-year-old Ellie shares the ups and downs of feelings in a single day: excited, grumpy, proud, worried, and many others. Encourages and models talking about and expressing feelings.

All My Feelings At Preschool: Nathan's Day

by Susan Levine Friedman and Susan Conlin
Readers share four-year-old Nathan's feelings and learn to express their own feelings as they spend a day with Nathan at preschool.
Ages 3-7, 32 pages, 7x8½, $5.95 paperback, illus.

Order Form

Name _____

Address _____

City _____ St. _____ Zip _____

Send payment to:
    Parenting Press, Inc., Dept. #305
    P.O. Box 75267
    Seattle, WA 98125

Or phone: 1-800-992-6657 (9-5 Pacific Time)

Prices subject to change.

Please send me:

_____ I'm Mad, 5.95
_____ I'm Proud, 5.95
_____ I'm Frustrated, 5.95
_____ I'm Furious, 5.95
_____ I'm Excited, 5.95
_____ I'm Scared, 5.95
_____ All My Feelings At Home, 5.95
_____ All My Feelings At Preschool, 5.95
_____ What Is A Feeling? 5.95

Shipping Costs	
Book Total	Add
$0-$20	$3.95
$20-$50	$4.95
$50-$100	$5.95

Book Total _____
Shipping _____
Tax (8.2% for WA) _____
Total _____